Copyright © 2018 by Diksha Pal Narayan
Author Diksha Pal Narayan
Illustrations by Abira Das

Published in Canada by:

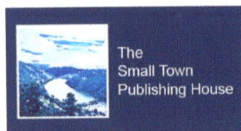

The
Small Town
Publishing House

First Printing September, 2018
ISBN-13: 978-0-9959398-2-0

Together, may we give our children the roots to grow
and the wings to fly.
-Author Unknown

Hi, Friends! My name is Ved and it's Hindu Heritage Month* here. I've learned so many things about being a Hindu this month. Would you like to know some amazing things I learned?

*The Province of Ontario, Canada proclaimed the month of October as Hindu Heritage Month.

2

Good Habits

Respect
your elders

Respect
your teachers

Respect Mother Earth

Respect your body

Keep your body clean

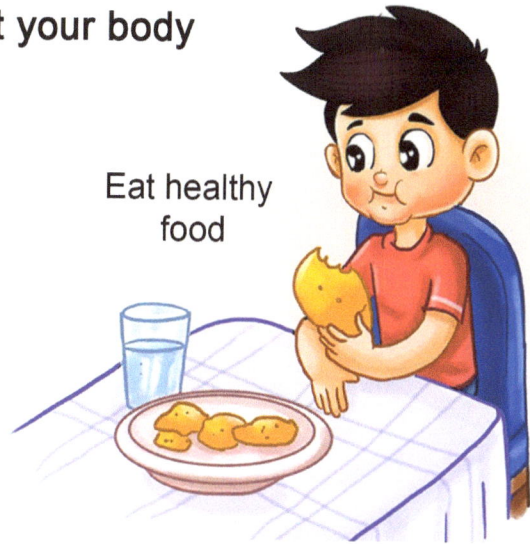

Eat healthy food

Limit your screen time

Keep your body active with exercise

FOOD BANK

Volunteer your time and be kind to everyone

4

Holy Books

RIGVEDA

SAMAVEDA

YAJURVEDA

ATHARVAVEDA

Vedas
are the books about
Hinduism

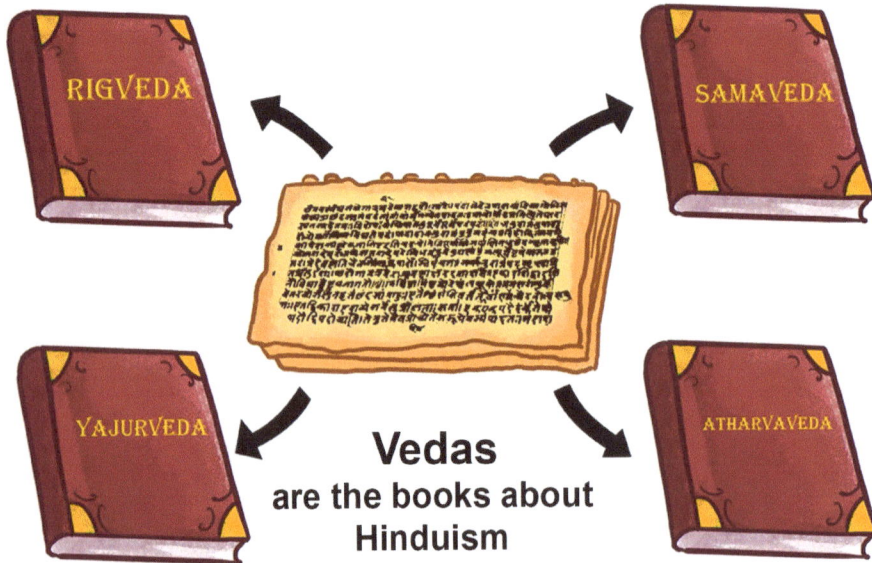

Ramayana
is the story of Ram, Sita, Hanuman
and Ravan

Ramayana

Mahabharatha
is the story of Pandavas and Kauravas

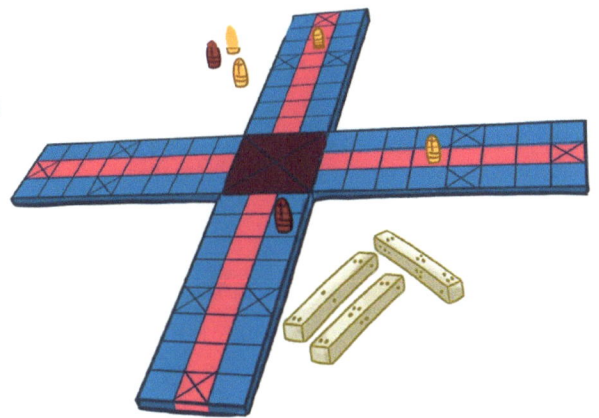

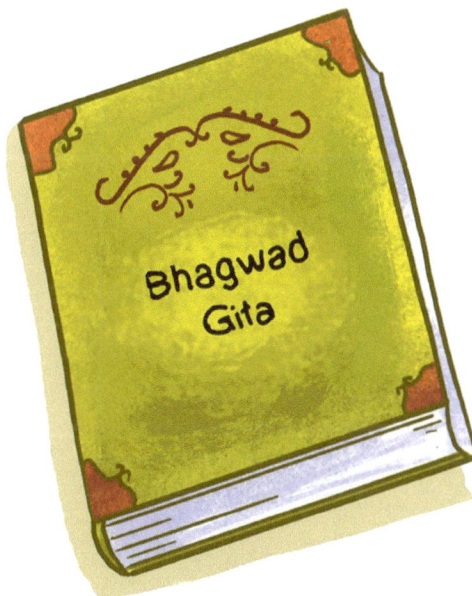

**The Bhagwad Gita is a
part of the Mahabharatha**

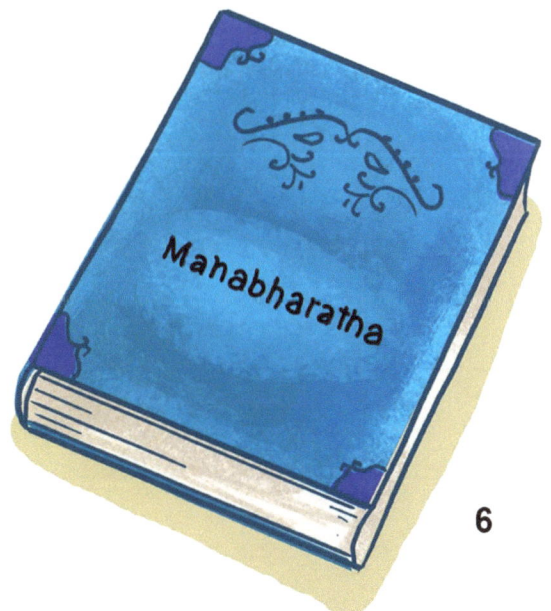

Hindu Gods

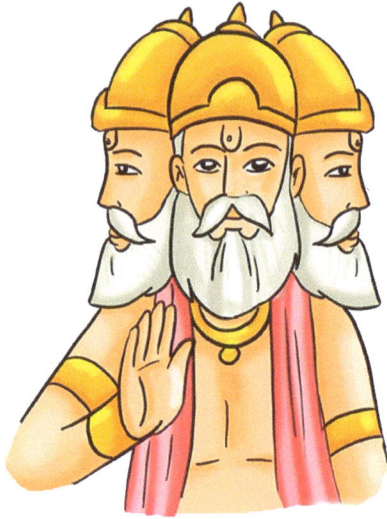

Brahma

Vishnu

Shiva

Parvathi

Ram   Sita

7

Ganesha

Krishna

Ayyappa

Venkateswara

Saraswathi

Lakshmi

Durga

Prayers

It is a good habit to be thankful, we can thank God by praying.
Some great times to pray are-

In the morning

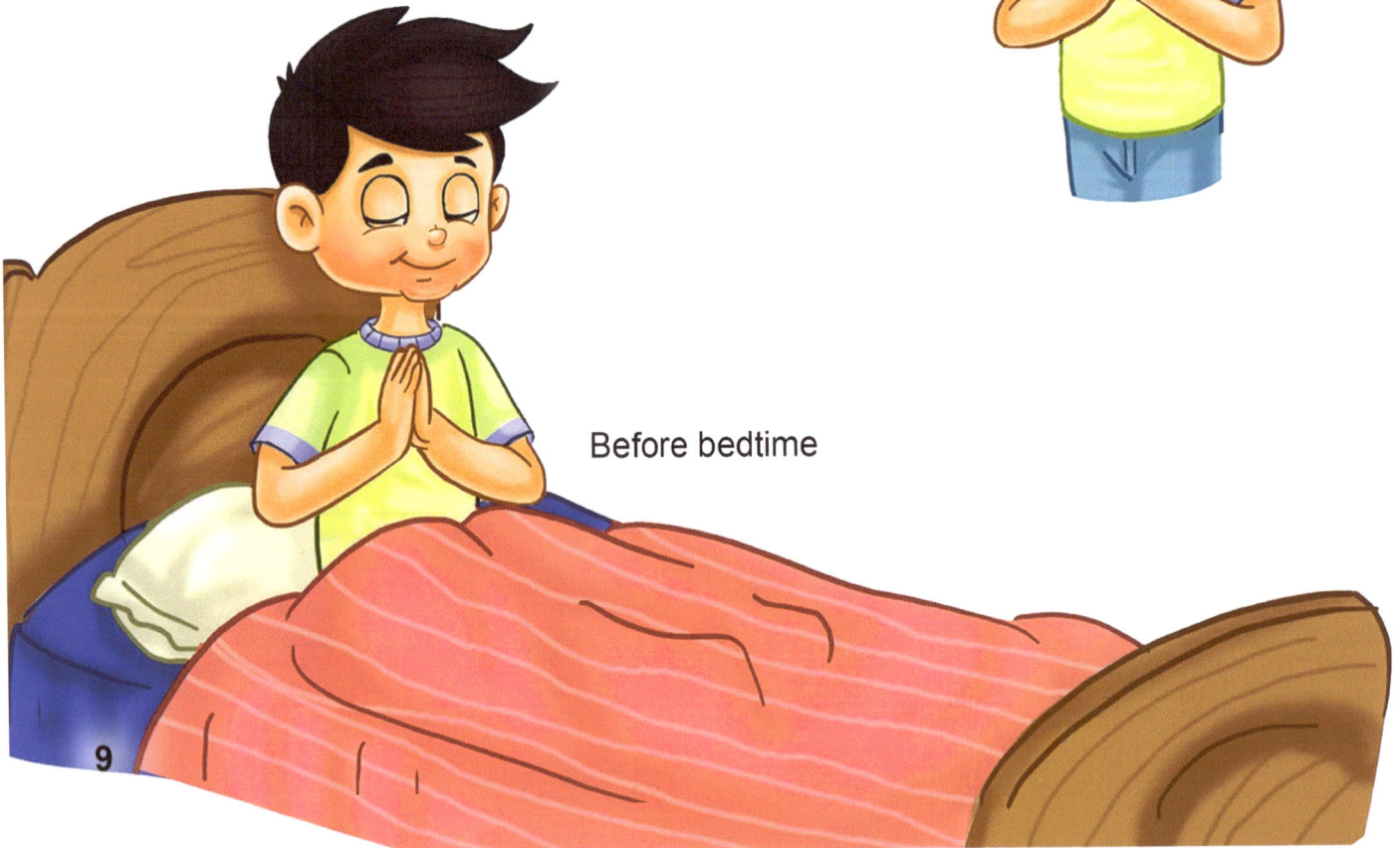

Before bedtime

Before meals

Before we study

Gāyatrī Mantra

ॐ भूर्भुवः स्वः,
तत्सवितुर्वरेण्यं।
भर्गोदेवस्य धीमहि,
धियो यो नः प्रचोदयात्।

Om bhūr bhuvah svaha
Tat-savitur-varenyam
Bhargo devasya dhīmahi
Dhiyo yo naha prachodayāt

Simple explanation: May the divine light of the
God make us smart and help us to walk on the path of righteousness.

Holy Symbols

Om

Swasthika

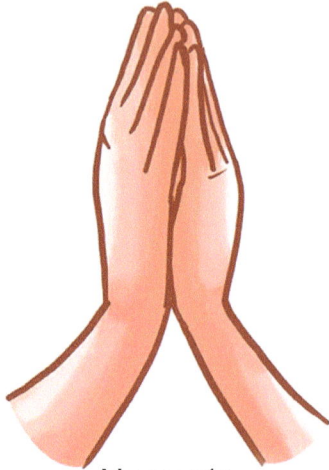

Namaste

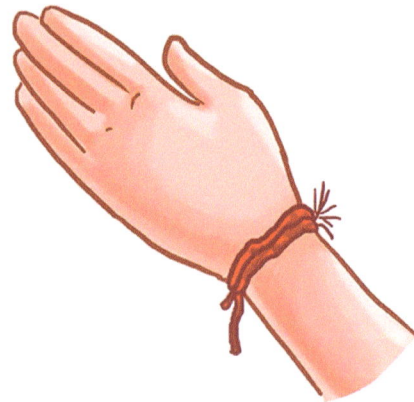

Raksha or Sacred Thread

Lotus Plant

Lakshmi Feet

Shivling

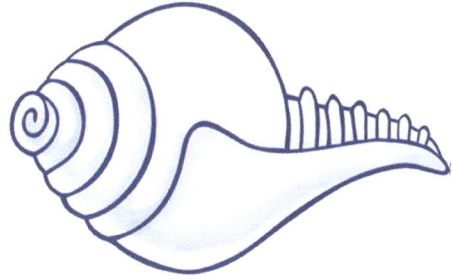

Shank

Rudraksh

Nandi Bail

Tulsi Plant

Cows

Temples

The place of worship is called Temple. In a temple you will find:

God's idol

Pandit ji

Agarbatti

Temple Bell

Diya

Pooja Thali

Prashad

Flowers

Festival Calendar
January

Makar Sankranthi

Pongal

Lohri

Maha Shivratri
February

March

Holi

Ugadi

Gudi Padwa

Ram Navami

Note: There are several Hindu festivals, and we have showcased some of them here. Dates of festivals change each year, so the calendar shows the sequence of the festivals and approximate months.

Festival Calendar
April

Tamil New Year

Baisakhi

Vishu

Bengali New Year

Bihu

Rath Yatra

June- July

Guru Purnima

August

Onam

Rakshabandhan

Note: There are several Hindu festivals, and we have showcased some of them here. Dates of festivals change each year, so the calendar shows the sequence of the festivals and approximate months.

Festival Calendar
September

Ganesh Chaturthi

Krishna Janmashthami

October

Golu

Navaratri

October**

Durga Puja

Dussehra

November**

Kali Puja

Narka Chaturdashi

Balipratipada

Diwali

Note: There are several Hindu festivals, and we have showcased some of them here. Dates of festivals change each year, so the calendar shows the sequence of the festivals and approximate months.
Check out the book **Ved and Friends Celebrate Dussehra and Diwali for all the reasons celebrated.

20

Traditional Clothing

We wear different kinds of clothing during festivals.

Bangles

Bindi

Payal

Nose Ring

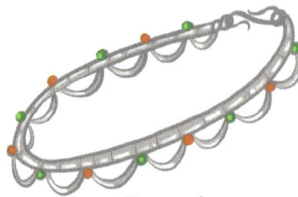

Toe Ring

Mangalsutra

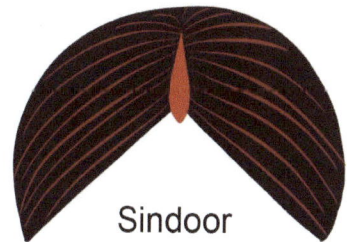
Tilak

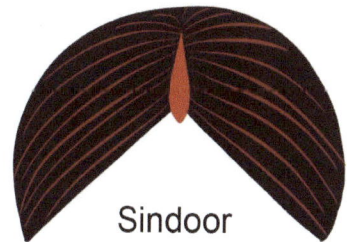
Sindoor

Important Ceremonies

Naming Ceremony

First Solid Food Ceremony

First Haircut Ceremony

Thread Ceremony

Wedding Ceremony

24

The 4 Stages of Hinduism

A Hindu's life can be seen in 4 stages

Brahmacharya

Learning is important.

Grihastha

Taking care of your family is awesome!

Vanaprastha

Being a grandparent is so much fun!

Sanyaas

Keep your body and mind healthy and continue volunteering.

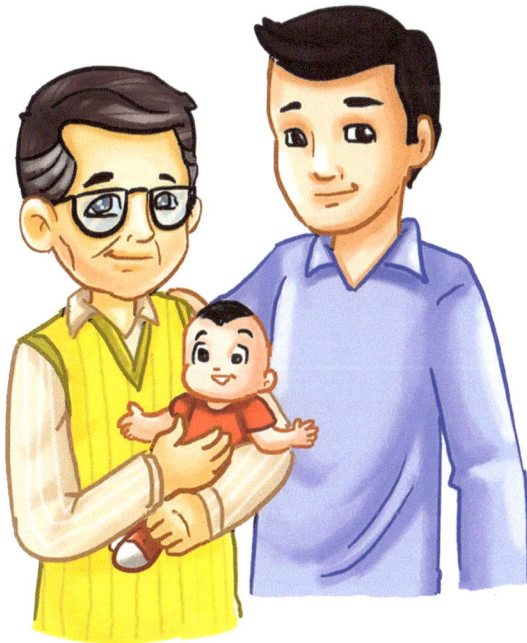

Healthy Mind & Body

Yoga and meditation are good for the body and the mind.

You should play everyday for at least an hour.

Let's try the Sun Salutation

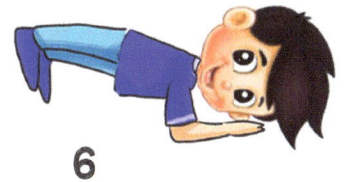

Ved- I follow some of these rituals
I learned this month.

Mommy- It's important to follow traditions,
but each family can decide on what traditions are
important to them. So you might follow some
traditions which might be different from what your
friends follow. Sometimes, you can make your own
traditions, too.

Daddy- Great job, Ved, you learned quite a bit!
But don't forget that you need to be a good
human being and be kind to everyone.

For Parents

Hinduism is one of the oldest religions in the world. With this book, we have tried to introduce Hinduism to our young readers.

Pg 3-4
Good Habits: As a good Hindu, it is essential to give importance to Dharma or duty or virtue. Respecting elders and teachers or Gurus is an important part of this.

Pg 5-6
Holy Books: Vedas are the oldest scriptures of Hinduism and are divided into 4 books or parts- Rig Veda, Samaveda, Yajurveda and Atharvaveda.

The **Mahabharata** is one of the two major Hindu epics of ancient India. The **Bhagwad Gita** is also a part of the Mahabharata. The Gita showcases a conversation between Lord Krishna and Prince Arjuna during the epic battle of Kurukshetra. In their conversation, Lord Krishna explains Dharma, Karma, Moksha and other important concepts of Hinduism.

The **Ramayana** is an ancient Hindu epic poem which narrates the story of Prince Ram and his struggles in the forest while in exile and his victory over the ten headed King, Ravan, who kidnapped his wife Sita.

Pg 7-8
There is a misconception that Hinduism has several Gods. The Hindu Gods are avatars of the supreme being. Some of them are reincarnations of the same Gods and Goddess. The Hindu trinity consists of **Brahma:** the Creator, **Vishnu:** the Preserver, and **Shiva:** the Destroyer.
Saraswathi: Goddess of Knowledge & the wife of Brahma.
Lakshmi: Goddess of Wealth & the wife of Vishnu.
Parvathi: Goddess of fertility, love and devotion & the wife of Shiva.
Durga: Is the Warrior Goddess, who is another form of Goddess Parvathi.
Ram: Seventh Avatar of God Vishnu and the main character of Ramayana.
Sita: Avatar of Goddess Lakshmi and the wife of Ram from the Ramayana.
Ganesha: The God who is considered the remover of obstacles also Shiva's & Parvathi's son.
Krishna: The most popular and loved avatar of Vishnu is the eighth Avatar Krishna.
Ayyappa: The God of Growth, he is the son of God Shiva and Mohini popular in Kerala, India.
Venkateswara: Is another name of God Vishnu, this name is popular in
Andhra Pradesh & Telangana states in India.

Pg 11- 12
Holy Symbols
Om: Most sacred mantra of Hinduism.
Swasthika: Motif symbolizing good fortune. The swastika symbol is commonly used before entrances or on doorways of homes or temples.
Raksha: Also called Kalava or mauli, is a sacred cotton thread (usually red in colour) worn to ward off evil from the person who wears the thread. Men and unmarried women wear it on their right wrist and married women on their left wrist.
Namaste: Is the Hindu greeting which means, 'The divine in me bows down to the divine in you'.
Lotus Plant: Also called Padma, has a special significance for God Vishnu and Brahma and Goddesses Lakhsmi and Saraswathi.
Lakshmi Feet: Symbol used to welcome Goddess Lakshmi, the goddess of wealth, into homes, by drawing her feet on the sides of doors of homes.
Shivling: Abstract representation of God Shiva, used in temples.

Shank: A Conch Shell is considered the trumpet of Hindu rituals. The sound of the shank symbolises the Om mantra. The shank has significance due to God Vishnu who is seen holding it.

Rudraksh: The rudraksh are prayer beads associated with God Shiva. They are large seeds of Elaeocarpus tree.

Nandi Bail: The bull calf (bail) called Nandi is the vehicle or ride of God Shiva.

Tulsi Plant: Holy Basil or Tulsi plant is the manifestation of the Goddess Tulsi.

Cow: Cows are considered sacred in Hinduism. In earlier times, cows played an important role in agricultural farming. They are also considered to be very gentle in nature, so have been given a 'caretaker' or maternal representation in Hindu scriptures.

Pg 13-14

In Temples, it is important to take off your shoes before you enter the actual place of worship. It is considered important you go with a clean heart, mind and body (hence take a bath before visiting a temple).

Pandit ji: Priest.

Prashad: Religious offering.

Diya: Small earthen oil lamp.

Agarbatti: Incense stick.

Pooja thali: Plate with all of the elements used to worship.

Pg 15-16

Festival Calendar

Please note this is the sequence in which most festivals fall, since the Hindu calendar is different from the Gregorian one, each year the dates changes and, subsequently, so will the months.

Makar Sankranthi & Lohri: Falls in the Hindu month of Makar and signifies arrival of longer days. Lohri is celebrated in Punjab and Haryana mainly, while it is celebrated in the Norther States of Inda as Makar Sankranti.

Pongal: Tamil Harvest Festival dedicated to Sun God. It lasts for 4 days.

Maha Shivratri: Is celebrated to honor God Shiva.

Holi: Holi is the Hindu Spring festival, or the festival of colours. It is linked to the story of Prahlad.

Ram Navami: Celebration of the birth of Lord Ram.

Hindu New Year is celebrated all across the globe by Hindus. The customs and traditions change with the region. Some of the New Years celebrations (first day of the **Hindu Lunisolar Calendar**) and their regions are listed below:

Ugadi: Andhra Pradesh and Telangana in India.

Gudi Padwa: Maharashtra in India.

Baisakhi: Punjab and Haryana in India.

Some of the New Year's celebrations (first day of the **Hindu Solar Calendar**) and their regions are listed below:

Tamil New Year: also called Puthuvarusham, is celebrated in Tamil Nadu (India), Sri Lanka, and many more countries.

Vishu: Kerala in India.

Bengali New Year: Pôhela Boishakh is celebrated by Hindus in West Bengal, Tripura and Assam in India and Bangladesh.

Bihu: There are 3 Bihu festivals celebrated during the year in Assam, India. The most important one is the Rongali Bihu which celebrates the spring festival and Assamese New Year.

Rath Yatra: Originates from Puri in the Indian state of Odisha. The festival commemorates Jagannath's annual visit to Gundicha Temple via Mausi Maa Temple (aunt's home) near Balagandi Chaka, Puri. The deity of Jagannath, is accompanied by his elder brother, Balabhadra, and younger sister, Subhadra, in the procession.

Guru Purnima: On this day, the author of the epic Mahabharta was born, his name is Veda Vyasa. On this day, students usually celebrate the day by thanking their Gurus or teachers for the knowledge and values they teach.

Onam: Is the festival of the Indian state of Kerala and tells the story of a just King Mahabali and how he keeps his word and honor.

Rakshabandhan: This festival has many legends to its history. In today's time, this festival is celebrated by brother's and sisters as a day of sibling love and affection where a sister ties a rakhi on her brothers hand and prays for his long life while the brother promises to take care of his sister.

Krishna Janmashthami: Celebration of the birth of Lord Krishna

Ganesh Chaturthi: This festival celebrates Lord Ganesha as the God of New Beginnings and the Remover of Obstacles. Some keep an idol in their homes for 10 days and offer prayers, after which, on the 10th day, they take the Ganesha idol in a procession and immerse it in a nearby body of water.

Golu**: During this festival dolls and figurines are put on display celebrating the autumn or fall season. This is an excellent time to socialize and visit relatives and friends. This festival is celebrated in the southern parts of India by various names.

Navaratri**: This festival originates in Gujarat, but now is a very popular festival all across the globe. Navratri also celebrates the autumn or fall season for 9 nights people gather and dance the garbha and dandiya raas.

Durga Puja**: This festival also coincides with the festivals of Golu and Navaratri. This festival marks the victory of Goddess Durga over the Demon Mahishasura, who she fought for 10 days.

Dussehra**: This festival marks the victory of Lord Ram where he successfully killed the 10-headed demon, King Ravan, and saved his wife, Sita.

Kali Puja**: This day coincides with Lakshmi Puja (Diwali main day). This festival celebrates Goddess Kali.

Narka Chaturdashi**: Marks the day that Demon King Narkasura is killed by God Krishna's wife Satyabhama.

Balipratipada**: On this day, King Mahabali (of the Onam story) comes to the surface of the earth to inspect his kingdom from the netherworld.

Diwali**: This day marks the return of Lord Ram with his wife, Sita, and brother, Lakshman, back to his Kingdom after having fought the battle with Ravan in Lanka.

Pg 21- 22
Traditional Clothing

We wear different kinds of clothing during festivals. The regional clothing of the South Asian Hindus changes from one place to the other. On page 21 and 22, we have showcased the 9 yard saree (Pg 21) and the normal 6 yard saree (Pg 22).

Tilak: Is a mark worn on the forehead during religious prayers or functions.

Some of the accessories worn by women and girls are generic like:
Bangles, Bindi (dot on forehead), Payal (anklet).
However some accessories are exclusive to **married women** like:
Toe ring, Mangal Sutra (sacred necklace worn by married women),
Sindoor (vermilion red powder put on the parting of the hair)

Pg 23- 24
Important Ceremonies

Naming Ceremony: During this ceremony, the baby is given his name that one calls him.

First solid food ceremony: In this ceremony, the baby eats his first solid food.

First Haircut Ceremony: The mundan ceremony is when the baby gets his first haircut, usually all the hair the baby is born with are removed and the baby is bald.

Thread Ceremony: This ceremony is performed for boys only, where 3 strands of thread are worn by the boy depicting 3 promises or vows- to respect knowledge, the parents, and the society.

Wedding Ceremony: In this ceremony, two people are wed as per Hindu rituals.

Pg 25-26
The 4 Stages of Hinduism
A Hindu's life can be seen in **4 stages or ashramas.**
Brahmacharya: Brahmacharya represented the bachelor student stage of life. This stage focused on education.
Grihastha: This stage referred to the individual's married life, with the duties of maintaining a household, raising a family, educating one's children, and leading a family-centred and a dharmic social life.
Vanaprastha: The retirement stage, where a person handed over household responsibilities to the next generation, took an advisory role, and gradually withdrew from the world.
Sanyaas: The stage was marked by renunciation of material desires and prejudices, represented by a state of disinterest and detachment from material life, generally without any meaningful property or home (Ascetic), and focussed on Moksha, peace and simple spiritual life.

Pg 27-28
Healthy Mind & Body
Yoga is the ancient combination of physical, mental and spiritual practices. There are wide variations to the form of yoga followed all across the world. The origination of Yoga was in India. Yoga helps in improving health and reduces stress, chronic pain, depression, and other diseases.
Meditation: Dhayana, or contemplation or meditation, is an integral part of Hindu tradition. It helps in reducing stress, anxiety and helps in growing self-aware.
Sun Salutation or Surya Namaskaar Starting Shloka:
॥ ॐ ध्येयः सदा सवित्र मण्डल मध्यवर्ती नारायण सरसिजा सनसन्नि विष्ः

Dhyey sada savitr mandalmadhyavarti, narayan sirsijasan sannivisht

केयूरवान मकरकुण्डलवान किरीटी हारी हिरण्मय वपुर धृतशंख चक्रः ॥

Keyurvaan makar kundalwan kireeti, hari hiranmay vpoordhrit shankh chakra
Simple Explanation: One should meditate to the form of Lord Narayana situated on the sun globe. He is seated on the lotus, with golden bracelets, crown, shark earrings; he is golden in complexion, and holds the shankha and chakra in his hands.

Surya Namskar Mantras

ॐ मित्राय नमः *Om mitrāya namah*
Simple Explanation: I submit myself to Him who is affectionate to all.
ॐ रवये नमः *Om ravayé namah*
Simple Explanation: I submit myself to Him who is the cause for change.
ॐ सूर्याय नमः *Om sūryāya namah*
Simple Explanation: I submit myself to Him who induces activity.
ॐ भानवे नमः *Om bhānavé namah*
Simple Explanation: I submit myself to Him who diffuses light.
ॐ खगय नमः *Om khagāya namah*
Simple Explanation: I submit myself to Him who moves in the sky.
ॐ पूष्णे नमः *Om pūṣṇé namah*
Simple Explanation: I submit myself to Him who nourishes all.

ॐ हिरण्यगर्भाय नमः *Om hiraṇyagarbhāya namah*
Simple Explanation: I submit myself to Him who contains everything.
ॐ मरीचये नमः *Om marīchayé namah*
Simple Explanation: I submit myself to Him who possesses rays.
ॐ आदित्याय नमः *Om ādityāya namah*
Simple Explanation: I submit myself to Him who is God of gods.
ॐ सवित्रे नमः *Om savitré namah*
Simple Explanation: I submit myself to Him who produces everything.
ॐ अर्काय नमः *Om arkāya namah*
Simple Explanation: I submit myself to Him who is fit to be worshipped
ॐ भास्कराय नमः *Om bhāskarāya namah*
Simple Explanation: I submit myself to Him who is the cause of lustre.

Sun Salutation or Surya Namaskaar Ending Shloka:
॥ आदित्यस्य नमस्कारन् ये कुर्वन्ति दिने दिने
Aadityasya namaskaran, ye kurvanti dine dine
आयुः प्रज्ञा बलम् वीर्यम् तेजस्तेशान् च जायते ॥
Aayu pragya balam veeryam, tejas tesha ch jaayate
Simple Explanation: One who does Surya Namaskar daily gets long life, intelligence, strength, courage, forever bliss and brilliance.

Some Prayer Options

Simple Prayer for God

त्वमेव माता, च पिता त्वमेव। त्वमेव बन्धु च सखा त्वमेव॥
त्वमेव विद्या च द्रविडम त्वमेव। त्वमेव सर्वम् मम्देवदेवा॥

Tvameva Mata Ch Pita Tvameva | Tvameva Bandhu-Ch
Sakha Tvameva | Tvameva Vidyaa Dravinnam Tvameva |
Tvameva Sarvam Mam Deva Deva ||

Simple explanation: O God, You are my mother, my father,
my brother, and my friend You are my knowledge and my only
wealth. You are everything to me and the God of all Gods

Simple Prayer for God (Sarva Mangal Mangalye)

सर्व मंगल मांगल्ये शिवे सर्वार्थ साधिके। शरण्ये त्र्यम्बके गौरी नारायणी नमोऽस्तुते॥

Sarva Mangala Mangalye, Sive Sarvartha Sadhike Saranye
Trayambike Gauri, Narayani Namostute

Simple explanation: Auspicious of the auspicious! Parvathi!
The fulfiller of the desires! Protector of all – Three eyed! Parvathi
Devi! Narayini! We salute your divinity!

Prayer during the Bath (Gange Cha Yamune Chaiva)

गंगे च यमुने चैव गोदावरी सरस्वती। नर्मदे सिन्धु काबेरी जलेस्मिन् सन्निधिं कुरु॥

Gange cha Yamune chaiva Godavari Saraswati |
Narmade Sindhu Kaveri jalesmin sannidhim kuru ||

Simple explanation: In this water, I invoke the presence of holy waters from
the rivers Ganga, Yamuna, Godavari, Saraswati, Narmada, Sindhu and Kaveri and
ask them to cleanse my body and my mind.

Prayer before starting studies (Saraswati Namastubhyam)

सरस्वति नमस्तुभ्यं वरदे कामरूपिणि। विद्यारम्भं करिष्यामि सिद्धिर्भवतु मे सदा॥

Sarasvati Namastubhyam Varade Kaama-Ruupinni |
Vidya[a-A]arambham Karissyaami Siddhir-Bhavatu Me Sadaa ||

Simple explanation: Oh Goddess Saraswathi, as I begin my studies,
please bless me with a lasting capacity for understanding.

Prayer before Food (Anna Grahan)

अन्न ग्रहण करने से पहले विचार मन में करना है किस हेतु से इस शरीर का रक्षण पोषण करना है
हे परमेश्वर एक प्रार्थना नित्य तुम्हारे चरणो में लग जाये तन मन धन मेरा विश्व धर्म की सेवा में

Anna grahan karne se pehle, vichar man mein karna hai; Kis hetu se is sharir ka rakshan
poshan karna hai; Hey parmeshwar, ek prarthana nitya tumhare charnon mein;
Lag jaaye tan man dhan mera, matr bhumi ki sewa mein.

Simple explanation: Before taking food, we need to think about the purpose for which
we want to save and grow our body. Oh, God! I pray that my body, wealth and mind should
always work for the service of Dharma.

Prayer at bedtime (Anjaneya Smarane Shlok)

रामस्कंदम हनुमंतम विनाथीयम व्रोकोडहरम सयनेषा स्मरेंथिथम धुस्पनम थस्या नैश्याथी।

Ramaskandam Hanumantham Vynatheyam Vrukodharam
Sayanesha Smarenithyam Dhuswapnam Thasya Nashyathi.

Simple explanation: We pray to all the brave Gods like Hanuman, Vynatheya or Garuda, and
Vrukodhara or Bhīma and ask them to wipe out bad dreams so we may have a peaceful sleep.

About the Author

Diksha Pal Narayan originally comes from a small Indian tourist retreat in the Himalayas called Nainital.
She moved to Canada in 2009.

She is a Canadian Journalist, who has contributed to the print and television industry in Canada and India. Diksha lives with her husband, Karthik, and son, Ved, in Milton, Ontario.

As a mother and journalist, Diksha wanted to use her expertise to make faith interesting and fun for her son.

With the changing times, there is a need to change our teaching techniques which also applies to our faith-based teachings. Diksha hopes that her books help make learning fun.
Her first book is
Ved and Friends Celebrate Dussehra and Diwali.

You can visit Diksha on the web at:
www.dikshapnarayan.com

About the Illustrator

Abira Das hails from Kolkata, West Bengal, India.
From a very early age, Abira was interested in the magical world of illustration and cartoons. In just half a decade, she has given vision and beautiful illustrations to over 150 books from all across the globe.

You can visit Abira on the web at:
www.abira-darkhues.blogspot.com

36

www.ingramcontent.com/pod-product-compliance
Lightning Source LLC
Chambersburg PA
CBHW040020050426
42452CB00002B/58